MW00457609

Steamboat's Osprey Family 2016

Bob Enever

Steamboat Springs, Colorado

This booklet is dedicated to

The Yampa River Botanic Park

whose board, staff, volunteers and visitors
took the osprey family to their hearts

All photographs are by the author
unless otherwise stated

Copies may be obtained from "Off the Beaten Path," a bookstore in Steamboat Springs, Colorado (SteamboatBooks.com),
from other good bookstores and at Amazon.com. Wholesale orders from C.Robert Enever (email: enever@comcast.net)

Summary

This booklet is the story of Steamboat's first family of ospreys in the 21st century. I am not aware of any record of ospreys nesting on the Yampa River before they were almost exterminated worldwide by pesticides in the 20th century, but there may have been.

The normal osprey routine is for a male to find a nesting site, an eligible female arrives, they engage in bonding activities and she constructs a nest. We first became aware of our pair on May 1, 2016, by which time some of these activities had already occurred. They went on to complete their courtship, enlarge the nest, copulate, then she laid eggs and sat on them. These activities were done quietly and unrecorded for about two months.

Things became interesting at the end of June, when their activities indicated that they may have a chick in the nest. At that time I started reporting nest activities in emails to friends and an ever-growing list of recipients. Attached to each email were a few photographs I had taken of the nest, at first from over 400 feet away at Trillium House, about level with the nest, and later from closer to the birds but lower.

Eventually three chicks were raised to maturity and all had migrated by mid-September. This booklet is more or less a summary of those emails and photographs.

 Note: I have used the word "chick" to mean the osprey young, from day-old chicks to fully-grown birds. At various stages they could more properly be called "nestlings", "young birds", "immatures", "first year", but "chick" is a short word and it avoids using several names for the same bird at different times.

Contents

How It All Began

I had been interested in putting up a platform for an osprey nest 20 years ago, and I knew just the place for it: on top of a long-abandoned aircraft navigation pole very close to the Yampa River and to the Yampa River Botanic Park. But at that time osprey were just coming out of endangered species status and the bureaucracies found all kinds of reasons why a platform should not be erected in an urban area close to a busy trail. Ospreys have since recovered worldwide.

The present effort started three years ago when Allan Reishus put up platforms in the Craig area and they were used by several breeding pairs of ospreys (see Allan's story on page 126). In October 2013, Allan kindly gave me a platform that he had on hand, but my "make it to last for 50 years" mindset required that I reinforce it, add three coats of paint and adjustable guy wires to secure the platform to the post during high winds. I used bolts to support the starter nest's willow branches, which were wired on.

Ernie Jenkins, who supervises parks for the City, took some of his own time to help me plan to raise this heavy platform 45 feet to the top of the pole. I rented a large hoist and Robbie Shine and Jeff Morehead installed the platform (their stories are on page 124).

Lifting and Securing the Platform

This photograph was taken on November 2, 2013 from 45 feet in the air and shows:

- the platform secured to the pole with its 'starter kit' of willow branches firmly wired to posts bolted through the plywood

- Robbie Shine, complete with ear-protection-muffs

- Emerald Field and beyond it the Fish Creek Falls area of the town and beyond that the already-snowy mountains of the Mt. Zirkel Range.

Jeff Morehead remembered to bring his camera with him and took this wonderful photo. (I will refer to Jeff Morehead as "Jeff" in this booklet).

Photo: Jeff Morehead

The Nest is Between the River and the Trail

The platform (tiny in this picture) sits on a post that was originally an antenna for Rocky Mountain Airways' ground control approach system, used to assist airplane navigation when landing at the Steamboat Airport in bad weather. Until the 1970s commercial flights flew right into Steamboat Springs. The manager of the City Airport in 2013 wrote that the system was obsolete and we could use the post.

It is ideally located: it overlooks the Yampa River, which is important to the osprey, it is only thirty feet from the City's Yampa River Core Trail that connects the 'Old Town' to the 'Mountain' so the public can see the nest, and it is close to the Botanic Park so we can keep track of what's going on at the nest. We knew there was a risk that pedestrian and bicycle traffic on the Trail might spook the birds, but on the other hand, we knew that if they could tolerate it we would all get to see their family grow. And tolerate it they did!

What a View of the Yampa River!

This is Jeff's picture, taken when they installed the platform, showing the bird's eye view of the Yampa River looking south from the nest. In the foreground is the Yampa River Botanic Park's Trillium House and beyond it are the homes of Fish Creek Mobile Home Park.

It is not clear from this photo, but one window of Trillium House has a fine, if distant, view of the nest.

Photo: Jeff Morehead

From the Nest Looking North

Only the birds get to see the Yampa River like this! Jeff's picture shows the north part of the island and the stretch of the river that runs close to River Road into Town.

We had this nice home for ospreys but no occupants came: not in the spring of 2014, not in the spring of 2015. Eventually we almost forgot about the nest sitting up there.

Photo: Jeff Morehead

May 1, Ospreys on the Nest

May 1, 2016, two and a half years from the placing of the platform: this was the day the Yampa River Botanic Park opened for the season. Jeff at home, received an excited early-morning phone call from Gayle Lehman, the Supervisor of the Park, saying that a pair of osprey were on the nest.

Jeff took his camera and there they were! Two handsome strong-looking ospreys who seemed settled in. They had already started adding to the nest.

We at the Botanic Park felt that the low volume of foot and bicycle traffic at that time of year would not frighten the birds but we were concerned that if the 'Steamboat Today' newspaper published news of their arrival (in 2013 it had reported on the Craig birds, but they were much further from people) it might draw noisy people staying around the nest, with the possibility of disturbance of the birds. Editor Lisa Schlichtman and Reporter Tom Ross cooperated. I kept Tom informed with weekly reports, and the 'Today' waited until July 6 to publish a low-key article, followed by a full page article on the ospreys on September 9 with a picture on the front page.

Other noises that could have frightened the ospreys were the nearby coal trains with their hootings, and truck traffic on US 40 and River Road, but this was a very determined pair of ospreys.

Photo: Jeff Morehead

Action!

May 1, continued. Later the same day Jeff was taking video footage of the pair flying around when he saw this seeming early attempt at copulation, or perhaps it was just part of the bonding activities. Jeff was able to freeze this still picture from his video footage.

Photo: Jeff Morehead

Sitting On Eggs

June 26, about two months after the arrival of the osprey: The new arrivals at the nest site had to make the nest complete in their eyes, because I gave them only a starter nest. The female did most of the nest-building. While this was going on the pair had to bond, with various displays that we know about but unfortunately did not see, including him bringing her a ceremonial fish, and her accepting it and him flying above her. They also had to copulate to fertilize the eggs. I had read from reports from other parts of the US that all of these activities would take about two months from the time of the birds' arrival at the nest.

After the first egg was laid, the female started sitting on eggs. Incubation takes about 5 to 6 weeks. The first egg laid is the first chick hatched, so the first chick has an enormous advantage over its siblings, right from the start.

The female sat on the eggs from mid-May till the end of June, at a time when the nest was exposed to occasional snows and strong winds, days of cold rain, and days of hot sun, with only short breaks during which the male sat on the eggs for her. This was arduous duty that took a lot of stamina.

Standing Guard

June 26, continued: while the female sat on the eggs the male was the guardian of the nest. There are enough bald eagle nests on the Yampa River that fly-byes were a daily occurrence and each eagle had to be confronted with a show of aggressive force sufficient to discourage any thoughts of raiding the nest. This perch on the opposite side of the river had good visibility up and down the river, so the male could see intruders coming. On occasion he would sit on the tall tower supporting the electric wires across the valley, looking tiny from the ground but in a great spot to swoop down on passing eagles.

The day the female started sitting on eggs, the male became the only provider for her and later the family until the chicks could fly and feed themselves.

Excitement! There's Something Going on Down There

June 28, from occasional observations I had calculated that June 30 was the last date we could expect eggs to hatch: today there was something in the bottom of the nest that caused both ospreys to show great interest. We observers were anticipating a possible hatching.

On this day I was excited enough to start writing a more-or-less weekly report with photographs of the activities in the osprey nest. I emailed these reports to Tom Litteral and Nancy Merrill, leaders of local birding activities, and to other friends and family in the US, UK and Australia. I received such warm and enthusiastic responses from those reports that I was encouraged to continue them, and they form the nucleus of this booklet.

The Miracle of Life

July 7, about 9 days since hatching: the two parents were seen fussing over 'something' in the nest. I had seen the female occasionally 'mantling', which hawks and eagles do to protect their prey. She seemed to be using her wings to protect 'something' from the midday sun, but we couldn't see what that 'something' was, until now. I was getting reports of two chicks in the nest but this photo was proof positive that there were two tiny chicks that she had been protecting. CHICKS! Everyone of us Botanic Park people was excited.

Now There Are Three

July 15, about 17 days after hatching: today for the first time I saw a third chick. All three appeared to be similar in size, so they must have hatched within a day or so of each other. One chick, obviously the first, was seen pushing itself forward to catch the first bite of any food that was going. If food was going to be scarce this chick would get all the food available, so at least one chick would survive. Darwinian logic of the wild is cruel and always at work.

The male brought fish, the female tore it into small pieces to feed the chicks. As soon as she had fed the chicks the male moved into the nest to keep the chicks warm while she ate her fill, stretched her wings and briefly flew around the neighborhood to retain her strength. When she returned, he went back to guarding the nest or went fishing. When the chicks were a little older the male no longer had to keep them warm while she fed.

How They've Grown in a Week!

July 21, about 23 days after hatching: the three chicks were developing feathers, had black marks on their faces and were growing rapidly. As the male had to spend more time away from the nest fishing for his growing family, the female started to take over the aggressive displays directed at any eagle, hawk or other osprey venturing near. Since the nest is so close to the river, and so much bird traffic flies up and down the river, almost anything larger than a swallow or cedar waxwing had to be confronted, intimidated and "seen off".

Four Hungry Mouths to Feed

July 24, about 26 days from hatching: the male had a full-time job catching enough fish for these four hungry mouths. Here he has dropped his catch and gone for more. The female has torn up the fish into small pieces suitable for small mouths and they're all lined up.

She held her wings out for balance when feeding the chicks because the wind blows much harder at treetop level than on the ground. Even so it was a challenge for her to place the food into those tiny mouths in a wind. When the three chicks had been fed the female fed herself.

Time for Housekeeping

July 31, this was about 33 days into the 50 days before we could expect the chicks to fly: the female had decided there was too much furniture; the chicks were growing and needed more space. The females do most of the nest building and it is incredible that this female could have lifted this heavy piece of wood 45 feet into the air, or that she thought that it was suitable nesting material. She tried, but did not actually get the piece pushed out of the way on this attempt; it remained balanced for several more days.

Looking Like Ospreys

July 31 continued: the three youngsters were starting to look something like ospreys. Here they and the female were all looking out to see, "where's Dad and the next meal of fish?" The female fed the chicks before herself, so she was perpetually hungry during this time. It appeared the first chick was now feeding itself from the bits of fish its mother had torn up; stage one of independence!

Botanic Park Staff and Visitors Watch the Ospreys

Jeff set up a telescope on a tripod inside a window of Trillium House. All through the summer Gayle and the Staff were able to 'take a peek' and they helped me keep track of what was going on in the nest. Many visitors to the Park heard about the 'scope and watched the birds through it.

Female Leaves the Nest for 3 Minutes

July 31 continued. This was the first time I had observed the female leaving the nest without the male being present, but I clocked her and she kept it short. Both parents arrived at and left the nest very quietly so as not to draw the attention of inquisitive eyes to the nest. Observe here how she dropped out of the nest and was already turning to go around the nearest tree and through the woods so she would first be seen by others far from the nest. When the male came in with fish he wound his way through the trees and swooped up to the nest at the last moment. They had good reason for this surreptitious behavior. I twice went to see another osprey nest ten miles upriver, on a telegraph pole out in the open, and on the second occasion it had been robbed of its two chicks, possibly by a golden eagle seen soaring nearby.

The Male Brings in a Morsel

July 31 continued: some of the things the male brought in were hard to recognize as food. Perhaps this was a crawfish or other crustacean held tightly in his claws.

The three healthy chicks were a testament to how good a provider he was. He also had to feed the female because she stopped feeding herself the day she started sitting eggs, and he continued providing for her until the family migrated.

Look at Those Talons!

August 6, about 40 days into the 50 days from hatching to flying: talons are the working tools of an osprey. They have adaptations to enable the bird to catch, carry and eat fish. Their talons have reversed scales which act as barbs to hold a struggling slippery fish. Also their third front outer claw normally goes forward but can go back to give two forward and two behind, the better to catch fish. During flight they adjust their foot to carry it pointing aerodynamically forward. To eat a fish on a branch, with one foot they hold the branch with the normal one claw back and three forward, but with the other foot they eat the fish with two claws each side (see the photo on page 107).

Ospreys use their talons to build nests and fight off other birds. The chicks use their talons to hold onto the nest while they flap their wings to practice flying, so they don't fall out of the nest to the ground, which would be fatal in the early days.

Female Brings in Dry Leaves

August 6 continued: we don't know why she thought it necessary to bring in dry leaves; perhaps she was just making the nest more comfortable. It was no small feat to find last fall's dead leaves in August.

A small fly-fishing class at Fetcher Pond was learning how to cast a line. Fetcher Pond is a small body of water near the Yampa River about half a mile from the nest. A member of the class, Monica Austin, had noticed a large mostly white bird flying in the neighborhood, but was concentrating on her rod and line. Suddenly there was a loud noise and splash immediately in front of the class and a large white and black bird emerged from the water carrying a fish in its talons. It shook the water off its wings and body as it flew and landed on a nearby pole. It stayed a short time then flew off. The male was draining his feathers before taking his fish home to share with the female and chicks; so the class got a close-up view of another way to catch fish.

Flapping Hard Enough to Fly

August 9, about 42 days from hatching: from what we knew it seemed that it would be only a week or so to the first bird flying. We surmised that the other chicks, hatched later and getting less food, might take longer to fly.

These chicks flapped so hard they seemed in danger of flying out of the nest and landing below before they were able to fly, but they must be genetically imprinted to hold on to nest-branches. After flapping they sometimes fell forward into the nest, almost upside-down: I chuckled many times.

The Male Brought Food and is Leaving

August 9 continued: these were truly splendid parents. The female was very attentive to the needs of the chicks, but kept herself fed and exercised. The male was so proud when he returned with a fish that he stood tall for several minutes, as if to take a bow, before taking off for more food.

Three Hot Chicks!

August 9 continued: on a hot afternoon in August three nearly-adult-looking chicks panted to dissipate their body heat.

I Wish I Could Fly!

August 11, this was about 44 days into the 50 days before flying: here was probably the first chick flapping hard. Its mother was keeping watch and looking down, perhaps at pedestrians on the trail below.

Still Flapping!

August 14, about 47 days since hatching: see the beautiful development of the first chick's wing feathers, outside and inside. It's almost impossible to believe that this gorgeous thing could have grown from an egg in 47 days. Six weeks! At six weeks from birth we humans have done very little growing.

Dad's Gone Fishin'

August 14, continued: note that the male baled out of the nest furtively, keeping low and through the trees until he was well away from the nest. This morning I was near the nest an hour before sunup, but the parents had already left, she for a brief exercise, he to get fish. As soon as the sun struck the nest, the chicks started flapping.

The male came with fish a half-hour later and left after the female had torn it up. I'm sure he must lose weight from this constant pressure to fish, fish, fish! When he migrates south he will only have to feed himself and can then recover from his busy summer on the Yampa River.

She did not look happy: she would have to wait for the next fish to get her meal.

This photograph clearly shows the two chicks visible on the left with white edges to their wing feathers contrasted with the two adults on the right with all-dark feathers. The chicks also have less dark on their heads and orange-ish patches on the backs of their heads.

Mother Feeds a Chick

August 14 continued: the first chick has not yet flown, but we are expecting it soon.

Mother Leaves the Nest

August 14 continued. The female furtively dropped out of sight and around the trees. She may have spotted an intruder from the nest and been going out to give chase, or she may have been taking a break from those perpetually-hungry chicks. Either way she was careful to take evasive action to protect the location of the nest.

You might have noticed the two poles sticking out from the nest. They were part of the design Allan used in Craig, but he didn't know why they were there. When the platform was installed they were dark brown (see pages 9, 17 & 19: brown from some paint I had lying around in 2013) but as the family grew they became mottled white. The parents, and the chicks from their earliest days, stood up to poop. They did this so forcefully that the "white paint" sailed well out from the nest, which is how the two poles became mottled white.

Its also worth noting that ospreys must have very strong stomachs to digest all those fish bones, which contributes to making their feces white. Other hawks and owls also consume the bones of their prey and usually have white feces.

Wanting to Fly

August 14 continued: whichever chick this is, it is flapping vigorously.

The Whole Family Together

August 14 continued: the chicks are up but the parents are resting. It's a hard life being the parents of three brats always hungry and continually frustrated at not being able to fly and leave the nest.

Others have alluded to the male feeding the whole family by himself throughout the whole time from when the female starts sitting on eggs until the last chick migrates, and it certainly seemed to be true based on my observations. I never saw her bring food to the nest and she ate on the nest, after the chicks. The female kept company with the last chick and cried until the male came with food, and this continued for another month until the family migrated out.

Mother and Three Chicks

August 15, about 48 days from hatching: the amazing thing about this photograph is that it was taken from near the bins in the Botanic Park and two of the chicks had both eyes intensely locked on me, the tall thing on two legs probably 100 feet away between the trees*. Ospreys' eyes magnify distant things extremely, so they could see me as well as if I was a few feet away. I was glad not to be a fish swimming a couple of feet below the surface of the Yampa River.

*The camera lens at 400 mm magnified them about 8 times and in the computer I enlarged them much more, so when looking at the photo it's easy to forget that they are so distant.

Mother Lands on the Nest

August 15 continued. The female can be identified by her stronger brown 'necklace'. As she landed she had the chicks' rapt attention: they are taking note of every move of her every feather so they can learn to fly like her.

Dad Goes Fishing While the Others Eat

August 20, about 53 days from hatching: our chicks may be a little late developing, but they seem strong and healthy.

Chick Practices Flying in Place

August 20 continued: this was the first time I had seen a chick in the air, not holding onto the nest. This is a big risk because the wind can carry it away from the nest and then it's fly or fall. Perhaps the chick's instincts tell it to take this risk only when there's no wind and when it can almost fly.

Family Togetherness

August 20 continued: this was that rare moment in a day when the male was not fishing, the chicks were not flapping and the female had not left the nest. However, one chick and its mother were crying for food, so the male would soon have to go fishing again. His wings were in the air, ready to fly.

I Can Fly!

August 23, about 56 days from hatching: this is later than normal, but our hatch date was guesswork based on slender evidence. To see the chicks flying for the first time is a big event to us, but to the chicks they have been training themselves for this in tiny increments since they emerged from their shells; it is just one part of their progress in life, with many more lessons to be learned in a short time.

.

Female Shows Them How to Take Off

August 23 continued: There seemed to be only two chicks on the nest, so the first chick may have been taking fishing lessons from its father. As the remaining chicks matured the female could give demonstration flights nearby so she could simultaneously teach the chicks, watch for predators and exercise herself, ready for the long distance flights of migration.

Flying Lessons Near the Nest

August 23, continued: the female was encouraging them to fly by example. A fast glide, with wings half-closed is one of many techniques they will need to learn, and is probably fun.

A Chick Flies Below the Trees

August 27, about 60 days from hatching:

To our surprise the chicks all took their first flights in the same week so we don't know whether this the first, second or third chick. It is remarkable that the male was able to keep them all so well fed that they all fledged at about the same time.

Chick Flies Up to an Empty Nest

August 27 continued: flying up to land is a learning experience, which you can see from the exaggerated spreading of the tail and primary wing feathers to stall onto the nest. The bird will soon learn to do its flying maneuvers with greater confidence.

This is the first time the nest has been empty since the chicks emerged from their shells two months ago. The photo was taken from near Trillium House, above the nest.

Osprey Chick and Hummingbird

August 27 continued: we'll never know, but the osprey chick and the hummingbird appeared to be looking at each other, each perhaps curious about the other.

The young osprey is distinguishable from its parents by the slightly golden patch on the back of its head.

The Male Flies Out for More Fish

August 27 continued: the female and at least two chicks are still dependent on the male for daily food. He shows such elegance in flight, with the classic bent-wing shape.

Chick Lands on an Empty Nest

August 27 continued: flying is the easy part, but just as with aircraft, landing is the hard part, and this chick has to land on a very small airfield. Full flaps and undercarriage down!

The nest is often empty these days because the parents and three chicks are out flying.

A Terrified Eagle?

August 28, about 61 days from hatching: I wish I could claim that I knew I was watching an osprey attacking a passing bald eagle, but no, I was taking pictures because there were a lot of big birds in the air and I shot what I could in haste through a narrow field of view in the telescopic lens. So this picture was pure luck. It's over-exposed and there's everything wrong with it EXCEPT that there's the osprey above and the bald eagle below with it's mouth open, as if in a cry, and it's head is turned up in apparent terror. It has probably been attacked every time it passed this way.

Eagles are a serious threat. Here is a link to a wonderful short video of a bald eagle taking a grown chick off a nest in Montana, recorded by a nest-cam:

http://www.audubon.org/news/this-rare-video-bald-eagle-attacking-osprey-nest-incredible-display-speed-and?s_src=20160819wingspan&utm_source=engagement&utm_medium=email&utm_campaign=20160819-wingspan

The Female Cries for Food for Herself and the Last Chick

August 29, about 62 days from hatching: the first chick learned to fish as soon as it could fly and the second chick soon after, but this one, the baby of the family, seemed to want to be fed all its life. These birds have quite distinct personalities.

However the parents want to migrate and their instincts seem to say they cannot migrate till the last chick can fish for its own food, so they are torn. The last chick may soon have to get hungry to be motivated to fish for itself.

The Last Chick is STILL Being Fed

August 30, about 63 days from hatching: the reports by others seem to stop when the first chick has flown, at about 50 days after hatching, as if that was the end of the nesting event. I think our first chick fledged at about 54 days after hatching and of course had a huge advantage over the others. But the last chick flew 6 days later, a great tribute to the parents.

We thought we had a crisis about this time: we could see only TWO chicks visiting the nest and wondered whether one had been killed, was lost or had migrated. A few days later we realized that the first chick had become independent: was catching its own fish and feeding itself on the branch of a nearby tree (see page 105).

Now only two chicks were at the nest each day, one was feeding itself on fish caught by the male and the other was catching its own. Both were still being protected by the adult female.

The Female Soars Above the River

September 7, about 71 days after hatching: the 6 foot wingspan of the adult female flying over the nest by the Yampa River on a clear day was a beautiful sight. She was still showing the young birds how it's done.

A Chick Carries in Its Fish

September 12, about 76 days after hatching: this bird was a tiny dot in the sky when first seen. It dived at very high speed to reveal itself as the second chick proudly carrying its own fish in approved streamline manner to the nest.

Lesson Learned

September 12, continued action from the previous page: here we see the chick flaring out to land on the nest. However, as soon as it touched down on the platform the last chick and the female came over to feed. This was the carrying chick's VERY OWN FISH and was definitely not what it had in mind, so it quickly took off and flew to a tree by the river to eat its prey.

Chick Brings in its Own Catch

Sept 12, continued: this is the first chick, which has proudly carried the fish it just caught to eat at its own roost. It did not permit its siblings to bring their catch to this tree to eat. I saw the second chick with a fish trying to land there but it was rejected and forced to fly around to find a not-nearly-as-suitable bough, which it used thereafter. These chicks have their own personalities.

Head First

Sept 12, continued: ospreys are said to take the head off a fish before eating it. When the male brought fish in for the family it always seemed to be missing the head. This ensured that he got at least something to eat on each trip. This chick has proudly brought its fish to the bough and the first thing it did was to tear the head off and eat it. This photo shows it having a very hard time getting such a large thing down its throat, but in a few more minutes it had swallowed the head.

Can a head be too big to swallow? Can a fish be too big to for an osprey to carry out of the water? I once saw a video of an osprey catching a fish that was too big to carry. It was in a lake and the osprey flapped a long way to shore trailing the fish beneath it. On our nest I saw how difficult it was for the male osprey to release fish he had brought in; he sometimes needed the female's help to unhook himself. From this I suspect that an osprey cannot release a heavy struggling fish once caught, so some may drown. That's probably why ospreys normally do not catch fish much above 12 inches.

Here you can clearly see that on the left foot the talons are two on each side of the fish as described on page 42, while on the right foot they are in the three forward and one back position, normal for birds.

A Happy Ending

Sept 12, continued. The first chick ate its own fish on its own bough and I believe that all three chicks caught and ate their own fish before they left: a very successful outcome for our osprey family.

After September 12 we did not see the adults, so they flew their own separate ways to wander the Caribbean and South America. We hope to see them again next year, but they live a violent life and take many risks just to catch their food every day. The birds are not tagged so we will never know.

Two of the chicks disappeared in the next day or two, we suppose also to travel their separate ways south. One chick, presumably the third, remained an additional couple of days, sitting on posts, perhaps learning to fish before it travelled. We understand that the surviving chicks will not return next summer, but perhaps in the summer after, then again in the spring of the third year, at that time looking for a nest site and a mate.

In most osprey families only one chick survives, sometimes two, but our 2016 parents brought up three healthy chicks, a testament to their courage fighting off eagles and to their organization: the male specializing in catching fish and guarding against predators, the female specializing in feeding and protecting the chicks. It's also a testament to the Colorado Department of Parks & Wildlife, which keeps the Yampa River and ponds stocked with fish.

****

By the Water's Edge

Photographs by Jeff Welton

Jeff Welton is a wildlife photographer and a native of Northwest Colorado. He says that when he can't find moose, elk, bear and foxes to photograph, he likes to go to the Yampa River Botanic Park to photograph hummingbirds, which he does beautifully. The following five pages feature Jeff Welton's photographs of the osprey chicks in the last few days before they migrated.

(photo opposite) "Let's Play in the Water"

On this day, Jeff saw the three chicks sitting on a branch overlooking the river and they were taking turns playing in the water. "Playing in the water" is part of the life-skills needed by an osprey. This appears to be before the first chick appropriated this branch for its own exclusive use.

"Someone has to go first"

This bird is about to land in the water to be the first to play.

Jeff Welton Photgraphy 2016

"This is Fun"

This bird, like a human child, is enjoying playing in the water.

Jeff Welton Photography 2016

"Dripping Wet"

Getting in the water is the easy part. Getting out is hard. Ospreys have to learn to overcome the immense drag of flying out of the water using their wings. Diving ducks, cormorants, grebes, loons all come to the surface before flying, but osprey fly out from beneath the surface, which requires many times the strength. The difficulty is compounded when they have to fly out of the water with a struggling fish, which can be large and heavy. The totally different skill of diving into water to catch fish seen from above requires on-the-job training, motivated by hunger.

"I'm Watching You"

This beautiful chick's wings may be spread for landing, taking off or just for balance. It is obviously curious about Jeff Welton's activities. Notice that its claws are in the normal three forward and one back position.

Jeff Welton Photography 2016

About Ospreys

Ospreys have a wingspan of 6 feet. Unlike any other hawk, their diet is almost exclusively fish; from fresh water or salt. They look for fish close to the surface and dive in feet-first, with their head against their talons, guiding them directly onto the target. They emerge with the fish and carry it head first to a roost or nest. Their success rate is estimated at better than one in four dives. Their feathers are oily so they do not absorb water, and they shake the water off their feathers as they rise from the water. They then usually sit on a tree or post for a few minutes to drain the rest of the water off, and perhaps to recover from the effort of catching the fish and flying it out of the water. Their main predator, the bald eagle, occupies the same waters and eats the same food. When opportunity presents, eagles will harass osprey to drop their fish, and will grab full-grown chicks. Our ospreys fiercely attacked any eagles near the nest and did not lose any chicks, or fish that we know of.

Ospreys are found near water almost worldwide. Ours are part of the American population that breeds in the North American summer and spends the rest of the year in Central and South America, much of it travelling. The exceptions are three small populations that are year-round residents of Florida, the Caribbean Islands and Baja California.

Maps of osprey movements in North America show a breeding range from Alaska and California to Labrador and Florida, but the biggest concentrations in the West are in the Rocky Mountains, Southern California, coastal Mexico and South Texas. There are also large concentrations around the Great Lakes, the East and South Coasts and the Caribbean. Their non-breeding range is around the Gulf of Mexico, Central America and across South America south to Buenos Aires and Santiago. There is no record of ospreys breeding in South America.

When they leave the nest, the males and females migrate separately, typically meeting again at the same nest a year later: it's a long-term relationship of sorts but they are still said to 'mate for life'. This is not unique behavior: Laysan albatrosses breed on Midway Island and when finished, go their separate ways across the far reaches of the Pacific Ocean before returning to the same partner on the same square yard of runway a year later.

The osprey chicks migrate separately from their parents and from each other: the survivors are likely to return to the same locality in two years, and again in three years, hoping to find a nest and find a mate.

An interesting question is whether the ospreys from here follow the Yampa, Green and Colorado Rivers to the Sea of Cortez on their migration, or whether they fly a direct route, requiring highly developed navigational skills and endurance.

Other Birds on the River

The ospreys share the river with other birds. These are part of their environment for five months, like the river itself and the fish, muskrats and otters that swim in it, the trees shrubs and grasses that line it and the humans that fish in it and tube on it. Following are some of the many birds often seen on the river.

Bald Eagle

Cedar Waxwing

American Dipper

Tree Swallow

Belted Kingfisher

Mallard Duck

Sandhill Crane

The People

Jeff Morehead (on the right)

Jeff is a dear friend who has been an enthusiastic supporter of the Yampa River Botanic Park since he first saw me working on it in 1995. I call him the 'Park's #1 Volunteer' because he lives his life around the Park for the 9 months of the year when the town doesn't live for snow. He works for the Park for far less than he could earn outside but in addition does countless hours of volunteer work and provides the Park with ingenious solutions to many problems. He lives next to the Park and makes it his backyard. He took college classes to learn how to create the Park's website and still takes classes to improve it. He has become a professional-level photographer and videographer. He didn't hesitate to go up in the hoist to secure the platform onto the post and he took the early photos of the ospreys.

Robbie Shine (on the left)

Robbie works as a leader in the City's Parks & Recreation Department's outside crew, and when assigned to work at the Yampa River Botanic Park has always done so enthusiastically. Before that he was a lead boatman rafting the Selway River in Idaho and fell in love with ospreys when he saw their reckless dives into turbulent waters to catch fish to feed their young.

Allan Reishus MD

Alan Reishus is a retired MD who lives in Craig, Colorado and was the first person to erect a platform and encourage the introduction (or re-introduction) of ospreys to the Yampa Valley. Here's his story:

"Why aren't there ospreys nesting in the Yampa Valley?" That was the question that came to me sometime in the early 2000's. I had marveled at the massive nests near Silverthorne and witnessed the spectacular dives of parent ospreys in Brown's Park National Wildlife Refuge. I had seen on my outdoor treks in the spring and fall, ospreys visiting the Yampa River corridor.

I contacted state biologists who said that they knew of no reason for a lack of breeding osprey except possibly the lack of nesting sites. As I read more about the birds and their nests I realized that if I didn't build a nest they would never come.

So I gathered plans for the nests and built two. The local electric cooperative offered two used 45 foot poles. Landowners along the river gave me permission to erect the poles. People volunteered, ready to assist. Most surprisingly, a local power line contractor agreed to erect the two towers at no charge. On a cold day in December 2009 the platform was erected.

(Allan Reishus MD, continued)

Two nesting seasons passed. In the Spring of 2012 one, then to my great joy another osprey appeared. That summer a single young bird was fledged. I watched over the nest and the young bird almost daily, like a nervous new dad.

The next year this nest and another were occupied and have been occupied for 4 consecutive years, fledging a total of 19 birds from those two nesting platforms.

Two more platforms were erected in 2013 and one was occupied in 2016, producing one chick.

With the nest in Steamboat added, the Yampa River is now home to a healthy and growing population of these fantastic fish hawks.

Photo by permission

The Yampa River Botanic Park

Mission: A place of serenity celebrating the trees, shrubs, plants and birds of the Yampa Valley

Unlike most botanic gardens, the Yampa River Botanic Park's mission includes bird-life. We provide many nesting boxes for tree swallows, we have a garden devoted to hummingbirds and treasure their nests, we have a display of the birds to be found in our area and we feed birds year-round. We enthusiastically supported the effort to bring a nesting pair of osprey to our part of the Yampa Valley.

About the Park

Gardening at 6,800 ft (2,000 m) in the mountains is a challenge. Winter snowfall in the Valley averages 180 inches (15 ft/4.6 meters) and blankets the ground from November to April. Annual precipitation of 24 inches (2 ft/70 cm) comes mostly as snow, with little summer rain. Winter temperatures get down to minus 30°F (minus 35°C) and summers may have only two months without a killing frost. The Park is in USDA Hardiness Zone 4. Preference is given to growing native species, but some high altitude and high latitude plants from other parts of the world thrive here. The Park has 500 trees and 60 gardens, many sponsored by individuals and organizations.

The Yampa River, for which the Park is named, runs from the Flattop Mountains at 12,000 ft (3,700 m) to its confluence with the Green River at 5,100 ft (1,600 m) in Dinosaur National Monument.

The Park charges no entrance fee because its operations are entirely funded by the voluntary contributions of its members and donors. No City funds are used but the City provides banking, office and vehicle maintenance work, creating a remarkable private/public partnership.

A parcel of flat land was donated to the City in 1992 by the author and his wife, who built the Park with their own money in 1995-7. It was opened to the public in 1997 and since the year 2000 has been managed by the Yampa River Botanic Park Association. This is a group of dedicated local citizens who work many volunteer hours to run the Park with a small staff.

Serenity Vision: An urban oasis, free from traffic, commercials and the engineered society. The design avoids straight lines, the paths twist and turn, the gardens are three-dimensional, the ponds are free-form and clusters of trees filter out the sounds of traffic.

Website: yampariverbotanicpark.org
Email: botanicpark@resortbroadband.com

PO Box 776269, Steamboat Springs, CO 80477
Tel: 970-846-5172

The Author

Bob Enever was born in 1928 near London, England. He had several business careers in Africa, Canada, Michigan and Steamboat Springs. He and his wife, Audrey have loved living in Steamboat Springs since 1971.

Photo: Holly Williams

About the Photographs

The osprey's platform is 4 feet by 4 feet and is 45 feet in the air, so you have to go some distance away, and higher to see what's going on inside the nest. This problem was acute when the chicks were tiny. About the only place to see them was from Trillium House, which is over 400 feet away and about the same elevation as the nest. I put my camera on a tripod on the patio for the early pictures. This location required "squeezing" the camera's sight lines between the leaves of overhanging trees when the wind wasn't blowing. The chicks were visible at first only when they came out from under the female to feed. The chicks were tiny specks in the film and I had to enlarge them many multiples to get what we got. When the chicks became larger it was less of a problem. From the west side of the Park, near the storage bins, the birds could be seen if they were on the east side of the nest, but could best be photographed in the mornings when the light was favorable. Near the end of the summer, I photographed from the walk between Trillium House and the Trail, and when photographing the birds flying along the river and near the nest I hand-held the camera. All but one of my photographs were taken with a Nikon 700 FX camera set at ISO 400, and almost all were with an 80-400 mm AF VR Nikkor lens without filters.